Roy Halladay

By Jeff Savage

AMAZING ATHLETES

⌐ Lerner Publications Company • Minneapolis

Lerner Publications Company
A division of Lerner Publishing Group, Inc.
241 First Avenue North
Minneapolis, MN 55401 U.S.A.

Website address: www.lernerbooks.com

Library of Congress Cataloging-in-Publication Data

Savage, Jeff, 1961–
    Roy Halladay / by Jeff Savage.
      p.   cm. — (Amazing athletes)
    Includes bibliographical references and index.
    ISBN 978–0–7613–7690–3 (lib. bdg. : alk. paper)
    1. Halladay, Roy, 1977—Juvenile literature. 2. Pitchers (Baseball)—United States—Biography—Juvenile literature. I. Title.
    GV865.H233S38 2011
    796.357092—dc22 [B]   2010043458

Manufactured in the United States of America
1 – BP – 12/31/10

TABLE OF CONTENTS

Roy wanted to pitch well
in his first playoff game.

PLAYOFF DREAM

Roy Halladay threw his first pitch of the game. Roy's Philadelphia Phillies were playing the Cincinnati Reds in the 2010 **National League (NL) Division Series**. The pitch was a 93-mile-per-hour **fastball**. Reds player Brandon Phillips swung and hit the ball to Phillies **shortstop** Jimmy Rollins. Rollins threw to first baseman Ryan Howard for the out. The pitch seemed simple enough. But for Roy, this was the pitch he had long dreamed of. After 12 years in **Major League Baseball (MLB)**, he was finally in his first **playoff** game.

A sellout crowd at Citizens Bank Park in Philadelphia expected Roy to dominate. Why not? He had been brilliant all season, winning 21 games with a career-high 219 strikeouts.

Though this was no ordinary game, Roy did what he usually does before pitching. He read from his favorite book. He solved a numbers puzzle. He talked about the upcoming game with catcher Carlos Ruiz and pitching coach Rich Dubee.

From the beginning of the game, Roy pounded the **strike zone**. He worked quickly between pitches. The first 14 batters never got a hit. The Reds were overmatched. The Phillies scored a run in the first inning to take a 1–0 lead. In the second inning, Roy hit a **single** into left field to drive in a run and make the score 2–0. Shane Victorino singled to score two more for a 4–0 lead.

Roy finally allowed a base runner in the fifth inning by walking Jay Bruce. But Drew Stubbs bounced out to end the inning. Roy retired (put out) three more batters in the sixth. Then he retired three more in the seventh. Then three more in the eighth. With one inning to go, he was throwing a **no-hitter**!

As the Phillies batted in the ninth inning, Roy sat quietly with his towel and water bottle. No one talked to him. He preferred to be left alone. He returned to the mound for the ninth inning. The crowd was on its feet, cheering like crazy.

Roy stayed calm during the game.

The first batter popped out to second baseman Chase Utley. The crowd roared and waved their white Fightin' Phils rally towels. Roy stayed focused. The next batter fouled out to third baseman Wilson Valdez. The final batter hit a tapper in front of the plate. Catcher Ruiz pounced on it and fired to first base in time! Roy had done it—a playoff no-hitter! "It's a dream come true," said Roy.

Roy hugs catcher Carlos Ruiz after throwing the last pitch of the game.

Roy grew up in Arvada, Colorado. Arvada is near Denver.

THE EXTRA THINGS

Harry Leroy Halladay was born on May 14, 1977, in Denver, Colorado. He grew up in nearby Arvada. His family called him Roy. His father, also named Roy, was a pilot. His mother, Linda, stayed home to raise Roy and the family's other two children, Merinda and Heather.

Baseball was Roy's passion. He played every position to learn which one he liked best. His father tucked him in bed at night. Together they talked about baseball. "Can you imagine what it would be like to be in the major leagues?" his dad would say. Roy would try to imagine it.

At the park, Roy's father threw him pitches. Roy enjoyed hitting. But he really liked pitching. In the basement of their house, Roy's dad built a pitching cage. It had a mound at one end and a tire and a mattress at the other. Roy threw fastballs through the tire into the mattress.

The practice paid off. Roy became one of the best pitchers in youth baseball. He took each game very seriously. After pitching, Roy's family took him swimming or kite flying to cool down. Roy's father kept Roy busy. "I never had a lot of time when I was just 'kicking rocks,' as my dad called it," Roy says.

In 1990, when Roy was 13, his father asked pitching expert Bus Campbell for help. Campbell had taught major-league pitchers, and he agreed to work with Roy twice a week. Campbell never asked for payment.

Bus Campbell worked with more than 200 baseball players in the Colorado area in his lifetime. He passed away in 2008 at the age of 87.

In high school, Roy focused on becoming a great pitcher.

Helping Roy was his reward. Before long, Roy thought of Campbell as his grandfather.

Roy joined the cross-country running team in high school. He played on the basketball team in the winter. But Roy's favorite sport was still baseball. As a pitcher, he developed a 90-mile-per-hour fastball and a tricky **curveball**.

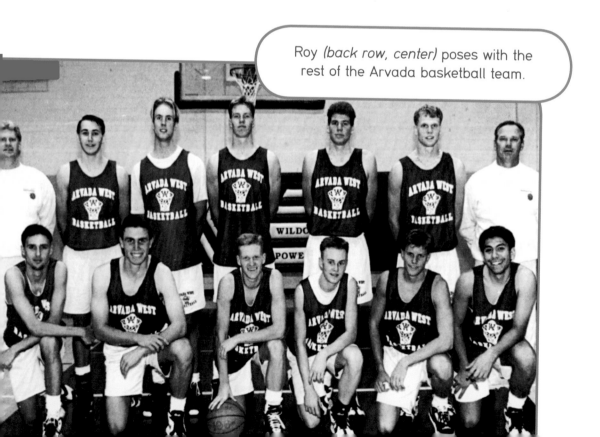

Roy *(back row, center)* poses with the rest of the Arvada basketball team.

Roy was named Colorado's Most Valuable Player in baseball in 1994 and again in 1995. When the team gathered for the bus trip for the 1995 state playoffs, Roy arrived limping with a cast on his leg. Coach Jim Capra was gripped with fear. Roy grinned and removed the fake cast. Roy was serious about pitching, but he liked to joke around too.

The Toronto Blue Jays selected Roy in the first round of the 1995 major-league **draft**. The Blue Jays paid Roy a bonus worth $895,000. Roy saved all the money, except to buy Bus Campbell a gift—a grandfather clock.

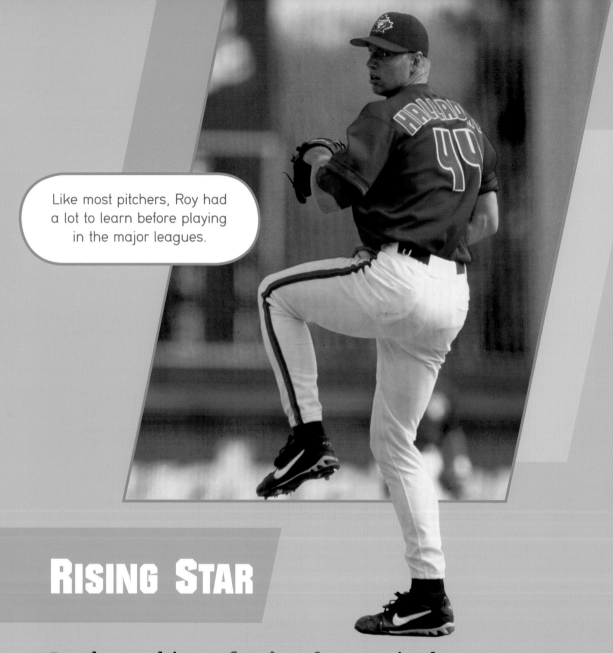

Like most pitchers, Roy had a lot to learn before playing in the major leagues.

RISING STAR

Roy began his **professional** career in the **minor leagues**. He spent his first two seasons in Dunedin, Florida, on **rookie league** and

Class A teams. Roy had reached the height of 6´6˝, tall even for a pro athlete. Minor league pitching coaches Scott Breeden and Mel Queen nicknamed him "Doc" for the famous gunslinger Doc Holliday. "It's better than being called Harry," Roy said.

In 1996, Roy led all Blue Jays minor leaguers with 15 wins. He was promoted to Class AA then Class AAA in 1997. In 1998, Roy got married to his wife, Brandy.

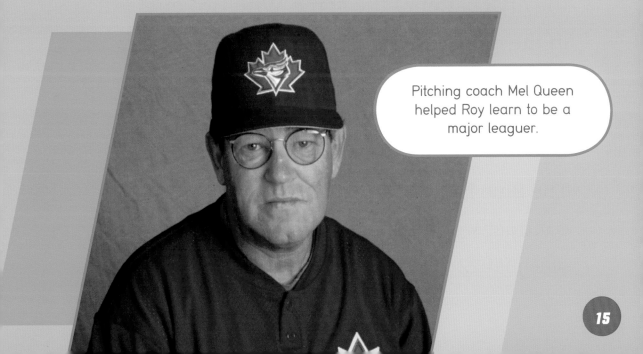

Pitching coach Mel Queen helped Roy learn to be a major leaguer.

When Roy pitched for the Blue Jays, he often invited children and their families from the Toronto Hospital for Sick Children. They would sit in "Doc's Box" at the Blue Jays' Rogers Centre.

Then in September he was called up to the big leagues. In Roy's first major-league start, against the Tampa Bay Rays, he struck out the first batter he faced. He allowed two runs in five innings.

Two weeks later, Roy made his second start. He did not allow a hit or a walk until the final batter of the game. With two outs in the ninth inning, the Detroit Tigers' Bobby Higginson hit a home run. Roy got the next batter out to win the game, 2–1. He pitched well in 1999 and finished with a record of 8–7. The Blue Jays rewarded him with a three-year contract worth $3.7 million. Roy was rich. He was just 22 years old.

Roy lost ground in 2000. His fastball still blazed at 95 miles per hour. But it came straight over the plate. Players learned to time it. They bashed hit after hit.

Roy's confidence was gone. Negative thoughts filled his head. "I can't bounce this pitch. I can't walk this guy. If I throw it over the plate, he's going to hit it 800 miles," Roy thought. In 19 games, his **earned run average (ERA)** was 10.64. For the 2001 season, the Blue Jays sent Roy back to the minors. But not just to Class AAA or AA. Roy was sent all the way back to Dunedin. He was told to start over.

The stadium in Dunedin, Florida, where Roy began the 2001 season.

STARTING OVER

Roy was confused. He sat with his wife, Brandy, in an apartment in Dunedin. They talked about what to do. Should he quit baseball? What about just going back home to Colorado? "I can never go home," Roy said. He was too embarrassed to do that.

Brandy went to a bookstore. She bought a book for Roy called *The Mental ABC's of Pitching*, by H. A. Dorfman. "I didn't understand the mental part of baseball," said Roy.

Roy met with pitching instructor Mel Queen in his office. "Doc, sit down. Keep your mouth shut, and just listen to me," Queen ordered. "Look at you! You're stupid! You have no guts!" Queen yelled at Roy to test him. Then the coach said, "If you want to pitch in the big leagues, you will do everything I tell you without question."

Roy practices fielding ground balls during spring training.

"OK," Roy said. "I'm ready."

Queen took Roy to the field for a lesson. They did not use a baseball. Queen changed Roy's throwing motion. Queen told Roy to throw with his arm closer to his side. The next day, they repeated the lesson. Roy tried his new motion with a ball. He noticed an improvement. Queen also changed Roy's grip on the ball. He taught Roy new pitches that sank and darted around the plate.

The changes worked. By July, he was back

Roy learned to pitch with a new arm angle.

in Toronto with the Blue Jays. He had command of tricky pitches that moved around the plate. He focused on each batter with positive thoughts.

By 2002 Roy was an **All-Star**. He won 19 games that season. Midway through 2003, he beat the Baltimore Orioles to win his 15th game in a row. He finished 22–7 and won the **Cy Young Award** as the top pitcher in the **American League (AL)**.

Roy had a hard time staying healthy in 2004. He still won eight games. But Toronto missed the playoffs.

In 2003, Roy started 36 games and allowed just 32 walks. He became only the second pitcher in baseball history to have fewer walks than starts while striking out more than 200 batters. The other pitcher was Cy Young himself, more than 100 years earlier.

Roy lies on the ground after being struck in the leg by the ball in 2005.

PERFECTION

Midway through the 2005 season, Roy had a 12–4 record. But then in a game against the Texas Rangers, Roy was struck in the leg by a ball. The impact of the ball broke his leg. Roy was lost for the season.

Roy came back in 2006. After that, he led the Blue Jays to three winning seasons. But each time, the team failed to reach the playoffs.

Roy throws a pitch against the Chicago White Sox during the 2007 season.

In 2009, the Blue Jays missed the playoffs yet again. Roy was frustrated. He had pitched 11 full seasons, but not a single playoff game. He loved Toronto. But he knew it was time to go.

Before the 2010 season, Roy accepted a trade to the Phillies. "I just couldn't pass it up," he said.

In Philadelphia, Roy was an instant star. He won on Opening Day against the Washington Nationals. He shut out the Atlanta Braves and New York Mets. His Phillies teammates were impressed.

Roy (right) holds his new Philadelphia Phillies jersey. He was excited for a fresh start.

Roy throws a pitch against the Florida Marlins on May 29, 2010.

"You want to talk, eat, sleep, and drink baseball? That's this guy," said pitcher Jamie Moyer.

On May 29, 2010, Roy pitched a **perfect game**. At Sun Life Stadium in Miami, he retired all 27 Florida Marlins batters in a row! This was just the 20th perfect game in major-league history. "It's hard to explain," Roy said. "But it's a great feeling."

After Roy pitched a perfect game against the Florida Marlins, he was presented with home plate as a gift. He gave it to his catcher, Carlos Ruiz. Later, he had engraved watches made for every player, coach, and team staff member. "I want to say 'Thank you,' because we did it together," Roy said.

Roy won 21 games for the Phillies. He was an easy choice for the NL Cy Young Award. Even better, the Phillies won their division. At last, he got to pitch in the playoffs. Roy seized the moment by becoming only the second player to throw a playoff no-hitter.

The Phillies swept the Reds in three games and moved on to face the San Francisco Giants in the National League Championship Series (NLCS). Roy pitched well in two games, but the Phillies lost the series in six games.

On days when he's not pitching, Roy sometimes flies model airplanes or helicopters around the locker room. But on a day when he is going to pitch, Roy goes into a zone. His teammates don't even say hello because they know he won't respond. "For me, the satisfaction is knowing you did something to the best of your ability," Roy says.

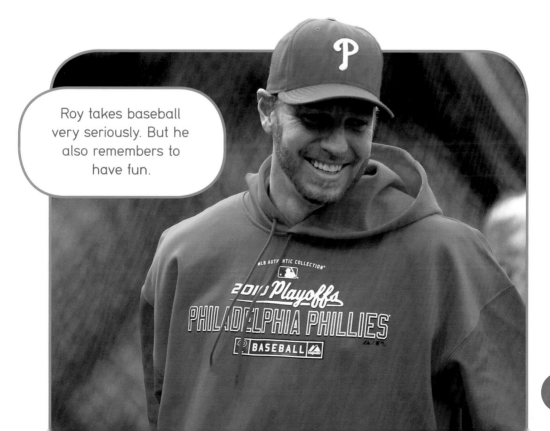

Roy takes baseball very seriously. But he also remembers to have fun.

Selected Career Highlights

2010   Won the National League Cy Young Award
Pitched the second no-hitter in playoff history
Named to the National League All-Star team
    for the first time
Led the National League
    in innings pitched
    (250.7) and wins (21)

2009   Named to the American League
    All-Star team for the sixth time
Made Blue Jays team-record seventh
    straight Opening Day start
Posted a 17–10 record with a 2.79
    earned run average

2008   Finished second in
    American League Cy Young
    Award voting
Named to the American League
    All-Star team for the fifth time
Won his 20th game on the final start of the season

2007   Named the American League Pitcher of the Month for April with 4–0
    record
Posted a 16–7 record with a 3.71 earned run average

2006   Named to the American League All-Star team for the fourth time
Posted a 16–5 record with a 3.19 earned run average

2005   Named to the American League All-Star team for the third time
Started with a 12–4 record before suffering a broken leg

2004   Won eight games despite being on the disabled list twice with a
    shoulder injury

2003   Won the American League Cy Young Award
Named to American League All-Star team for the second time
Posted a 22–7 record with a 3.25 earned run average
Pitched the first extra-inning (10 innings) shutout in the major
    leagues since 1991

2002   Named to the American League All-Star team for the first time
Led Blue Jays starters with a 19–7 record and a 2.93 earned run
    average

1999   Posted a winning record (8–7) in his first full season in the majors

1998   Promoted to the major leagues
In his second career start, had a no-hitter broken up with two outs in the ninth inning

1997   Won nine games in the minor leagues

1996   Led all Blue Jays minor leaguers in wins (15)

1995   Selected in the first round of the major-league draft by the Toronto Blue Jays
As a high school senior, was named All-Conference, All-State, and State Most Valuable Player

1994   As a high school junior, was named All-Conference, All-State, and State Most Valuable Player

1993   As a high school sophomore, was named to All-Conference and All-State teams

Glossary

All-Star: one of a group of the best major-league players, as voted by fans, who meet in a special game played in July

American League (AL): one of Major League Baseball's two leagues. The AL has 14 teams, including the Toronto Blue Jays, the New York Yankees, the Baltimore Orioles, the Oakland Athletics, the Minnesota Twins, and others.

curveball: a type of pitch with a spin that causes a curving motion

Cy Young Award: an award given each year to the top pitchers of the American League and the National League, as voted by the media

Division Series: the first round of Major League Baseball's playoffs. Teams play a five-game series. The first team to win three games moves on to the League Championship Series.

draft: a yearly event in which professional teams take turns choosing new players from a selected group

earned run average (ERA): the number of runs a pitcher allows per nine innings. For example, if a pitcher pitches nine innings and gives up three runs, the pitcher's ERA would be 3.00.

fastball: a fast pitch that usually travels straight

home run: a hit that allows a batter to circle all the bases and score

Major League Baseball (MLB): the top level of professional baseball. MLB is divided into the National League and the American League.

minor leagues: a group of teams where players work to improve their skills in hopes of moving up to the major leagues

National League (NL): one of MLB's two leagues. The NL has 16 teams, including the San Francisco Giants, the New York Mets, the Atlanta Braves, the Washington Nationals, the Florida Marlins, and others.

no-hitter: a baseball game that goes at least nine innings in which no opposing player gets a hit

perfect game: a baseball game that goes at least nine innings in which no opposing player reaches base

playoff: a game in a series played after a regular season to determine a champion

professional: an athlete who is paid to compete in sports

rookie league: a minor league for players in their first season

shortstop: a player who plays in the field between second and third base

single: a hit that allows the batter to reach first base

strike zone: the square area above home plate, generally between both sides and between the batter's knees and chest

Further Reading & Websites

Donovan, Sandy. *Derek Jeter*. Minneapolis: Lerner Publications Company, 2011.

Jackson, Dave. *Philadelphia Phillies*. Edina, MN: Abdo Publishing Company, 2011.

Kelley, K. C. *Philadelphia Phillies*. Mankato, MN: Child's World, 2010.

Savage, Jeff. *Ryan Howard*. Minneapolis: Lerner Publications Company, 2009.

The Official Site of Major League Baseball
http://www.mlb.com
Major League Baseball's official website provides fans with the latest scores and game schedules, as well as statistics and biographies of players.

Philadelphia Phillies: The Official Site
http://www.philadelphiaphillies.com
The official website of the Philadelphia Phillies includes the team schedule and game results, late-breaking news, biographies of Roy Halladay and other players, and much more.

Sports Illustrated Kids
http://www.sikids.com
The *Sports Illustrated Kids* website covers all sports, including baseball.

Index

Photo Acknowledgments

The images in this book are used with the permission of: AP Photo/Matt
Slocum, pp. 4, 8; © Jeff Zelevansky/Getty Images, pp. 7, 27; © Steve Krull
Autumn Color Images/Alamy, p. 9; Seth Poppel Yearbook Library, pp. 11,
12; © Scott Halleran/Getty Images, pp. 14, 15; REUTERS/Str Old, p. 17; © Al
Messerschmidt Archive/Getty Images, p. 18; REUTERS/Colin Braley, p. 19;
REUTERS/Ron Kuntz, p. 20; AP Photo/David Pellerin, p. 22; AP Photo/Nathan
Denette, CP, p. 23; REUTERS/Tim Shaffer, p. 24; © Robert Vigon/Florida
Marlins/MLB Photos via Getty Images, p. 25; © Ezra Shaw/Getty Images, p. 28.

Front cover: © Jim McIsaac/Getty Images.